Bearing the Body of Hector Home

_____

Robert Cooperman

FUTURECYCLE PRESS
www.futurecycle.org

Cover artwork, painting by Gene McCormick; cover and interior design by Diane Kistner; Minion Pro text and Jost titling

Library of Congress Control Number: 2022944644

Published by FutureCycle Press
Athens, Georgia, USA

ISBN 978-1-952593-35-2

As always, for Beth,
who makes it all a glorious journey

Contents

Prologue

Hector's Spirit, While Achilles Drags His Corpse
  Around the Walls of Troy..9

Part I—The Rage of Achilles

Achilles Rages Over Hector's Corpse..13
Hector's Ghost Hovers by Achilles' Tent...14
Briseis, Achilles' Concubine...15
Idreus, Priam's Herald, Accompanies His Master
  to the Tent of Achilles...16
Achilles Returns Hector's Body...17
From His Tent, Odysseus Watches Priam
  Take His Son's Body Back to Troy...18
Briseis to Neoptolemus, Son of Achilles:
  As Priam Leaves with Hector's Body...19
Melandros, Menelaus' Charioteer, As Priam Leaves
  with Hector's Body...20
Menelaus Confronts Achilles After the Latter Returns
  Hector's Body to Priam...21
Agamemnon Joins His Brother Menelaus in Arguing with Achilles.........22
Achilles Confronts Agamemnon and Menelaus.....................................23
Diomedes Watches Achilles, Agamemnon, and Menelaus Argue..............24
Nestor Watches Priam Drive Off with the Body of Hector.....................25
Thersites, an Achaean Foot Soldier, Watches Priam
  Leave with Hector's Body..26

Part II—The Lonely Road Back to Troy

Priam, on His Way Back to Troy with Hector's Body,
  Thinks of Achilles..29
Verax, a Mule Cart Driver, Upon the Return
  of Priam with Hector's Body..30
Tul the Butcher, as Priam Returns with Hector's Body..........................31
Threnia, a Prostitute, As Hector's Body Is Brought Back to Troy............32
Andromache Silently Addresses Hecuba...33
Galatea, a Prostitute, Watches the Body of Hector
  Taken to Its Pyre...34
Timal, a Woodcutter, Before the Funeral Rites for Hector Begin.............35

Part III—At the Funeral Rites

Jezrius, Court Astrologer and High Priest,
  Begins the Funeral Rites for Hector..39
Selene, Daughter of the Court Astrologer..40
Matax the Pickpocket..41
Cassandra, at Her Brother Hector's Funeral Rites...........................42
Drabo, a Trojan Tax Collector..43
Trebia, the Mother of a Slain Foot Soldier......................................44
Zythum, a Crippled War Veteran, Begging at the Funeral Rites.......45
Blena, a War Widow..46
Hippomanes, Hector's Horse Breaker...47
Laocoon, Chief of Security, at the Funeral Rites..............................48
During Hector's Funeral Service, Massopius Tries
  To Escape from Troy..49
Gigantes, a Guard at One of the Secret
  Passageways in Troy's Wall...50
Cryptoros, a Greek Spy, at the Funeral Rites....................................51
Pyrates, Master Armorer..52
Ilex, the Royal Chef...53
Majestius, Court Magician...54
Dinaros, a Second Beggar..55
Pepella and Her New Husband, a Butcher..56
Crillus, a Dead Trojan Foot Soldier
  and Brother to Baicus the Tavern Owner.......................................57
Memna, Wife of the Tavern Owner Baicus.......................................58
After the Funeral, the Tavern Owner Baicus
  Thinks About His Wife and Dead Brother......................................59
Priam's Prayer: The Last Day of Mourning......................................60
Hecuba Answers Priam's Plea to Their Dead Son Hector................61
Andromache, on the Last Day of Mourning.....................................62
Trema, Servant to Andromache...63
After Andromache's Outburst, Cassandra Holds Astayanax.............64

Part IV—The War Goes On

After the Funeral Rites, the Deserter Threnon Faces Execution.......67
Bathyros, Hector's Former Squire..68
Kallindros, Hector's Chariot Driver...69
Adriana, Helen's Maid..70
Limnos, Paris' Servant, After the Days of Mourning........................71

Epilogue

The Ghost of Hector Bids Farewell..75

Prologue

Hector's Spirit, While Achilles Drags His Corpse Around the Walls of Troy

I could not face him, but ran, as a hare
tries to dodge the snapping jaws of a wolf.
In the end, I couldn't run fast enough.
Now as I hover above Ilium,
Achilles kicks me, pierces my ankles,
drags me around Troy, to desecrate me,
and deny me the pyre's oblivion.

You'd think I'd rage to escape my shameful fear.
Strangely, I prefer it here: free to drift
beside my wife, though I can no longer
shelter her within my caressing arms.
At least I can form a chrysalis mist
she'll perhaps notice and take succor in.
And here's my father and mother, sobbing.
Maybe they'll sense me and find some solace.

But wondrous, my son Astayanax reaches
for my ghostly breastplate, my wraith-thin helmet.
How I long to take my boy in my arms
and assure him that he'll be safe and well;
then toss and catch him from the joyous air.

No, I don't want to forget: my nostrils
filled with the heavy smell of horse manure;
the aromas of roasting ox and pig;
the heady stench of my wife's ecstasies;
the stink of fear, when my chariot thundered,
Greeks pissing terror when my sword slashed them,
as Achilles played on my sulfur trembling:

the only warrior who could best me,
our fates ivy strands twined onto a wall.
I go on ahead, but you won't be long
in following me to the Halls of Death.
But now, let me take in—for the last time—
all I have loved and all who have loved me.

Part I—The Rage of Achilles

Achilles Rages Over Hector's Corpse

You died too easy, cheating me of hand-
to-hand combat to last all blood-bathed day.
I longed to feel the storm-wind of your sword
pass over me when I ducked and parried,
my sword slashing your shield like crashing boulders,
the clang of my bronze against your helmet,
the thud of my shield blocking your thick blade,
your cry of shock and anguish when my sword
pierced your breastplate, your blood like the spring spate.

I wanted to sweat and shout and grow parched
as we traded blows upon blows, from dawn
through mid-day; and finally as the sun-god
was whipping his team for his nightly rest
below the ramparts of Troy, your vile head
would fly off, my arms almost too sore
and exhausted to strike another blow.

You dog masquerading as a hero,
if you'd given a decent accounting,
I'd spare you now this humiliation
of piercing your ankles and tying you
to the rear axle of my chariot
and dragging you around Troy's walls to strike
despair in the hearts of all those within:
as a hurricane reduces sailors
to blubbering prayers while they shit themselves,
and the monster wave smashes down on them
like the talons of a giant griffon.

I'll cut off your hands, so you can't present
the Ferryman the necessary coin.
I'll slice off your wee pizzle and toss it
to the wraith-curs that haunt this battlefield.
Troy's best warrior? The gods must think us
weaklings, to take so long to defeat you.

Hector's Ghost Hovers by Achilles' Tent

Yes, slash me, take a mallet to my face,
drag me face-down around the walls of Troy,
deny me my rightful pyre, my parents
the solace of my death rites. We both know
you'll release my body when Father begs
and pours treasures for you like casks of wine.

He'll speak of your beloved Patroclus,
and how he was cremated with honor;
he'll lament his war-lost sons. You'll both weep
and, finally, I'll be done with this Earth.

At first, it amused me to see you try
to tear at my corpse in your tantrum spasms,
as it filled me with brief joy to behold
my wife, my son, dear parents, even Paris—
selfish as a vulture hoarding entrails—
even Helen, gorgeous as a viper.

But now it's time for you to release me.
Ah, here comes Father, shrouded in mist,
steering his donkey cart, heavy-hearted
as Niobe, turned to stone by the grief
of seeing each of her children struck down.

Once I've crossed to Styx's far shore,
your Patroclus and I will greet each other
as if comrades in arms, then we'll forget
this war, the dead forgetting everything.

Briseis, Achilles' Concubine

Great Hector? Let him rot; let Priam's tears
turn to knives and stab the old man's eyes out,
for when I reached womanhood in his court,
he would press against me, smirk I'd bear more
spawn than already swarmed his palace suites.

When I'd cringe, he'd laugh, "Your loyal Father
will frolic at the idea like a colt
prancing in a pasture heady with clover."
Though I wanted even less of Priam
than I do of other men, I suffer
Achilles: unthreatening as a mouse.
for all his prowess on the battlefield.
When he does take me, it's gentle surf,
not Agamemnon's sail-shearing typhoons.

And though Hector never sought to have me,
he never tried to stop his goat-Papa,
Hector deaf to my begging, drawing back
from me as if I were a pariah,
a leper, soiled by Priam's filthy seed.

When the Danaans captured me, I rejoiced,
for Achilles sensed I preferred women,
as I could tell it was men he adored:
he and Patroclus wedded at the heart,
more devoted than wolves that mate for life.
He always came to me with apologies,
sighing he needed a release from battle:
all those souls he'd sent to Hades with no coin
weighing on him like Sisyphus' stone.
Now sorrow grips him like a hawk's talons,
with his dear Patroclus dead, and Hector's
corpse a pitiful vessel of revenge.

Like all the women of my clan, I see
wraiths when they mist up and shimmer like silks;
like Patroclus now, begging Achilles
to return Hector, though I shout, "Never!"

Idreus, Priam's Herald, Accompanies His Master to the Tent of Achilles

The fog this cart creaks through is moth-gauzy
as Helen's robes, flaunting herself before
the stunned court, daring us all to hiss, "Vile slut!"
This mist won't hide us, but my Lord Priam
will no more be deterred from reclaiming
Hector's corpse than a hare can kill a wolf.

I know a father's grief, but I'd have left
Hector to rot: to him, I was a fop,
not one who knew to dress in robes
so resplendent as to insure houndish
obedience and awe to King Priam
when I struck my staff of office against
the marble floor: silence a huge curtain.

Hector knew me less than the wind knows a pine:
not that my dear wife died of a fever—
I hid my grief to perform my duty—
nor that my son was so ground up by Greek
hooves I knew him only by a birthmark.

Nor did Hector realize Priam treasured
my advice: nodding, whispering, "Just so."
Only once he turned deaf: this suicide
trek to reclaim his son from Achilles.
We'll both be taken hostage, or slaughtered,
Priam's loss more catastrophic than Hector's:
without the King, the walls will fall before
those invaders can breach our proud ramparts.

Say that I fear being killed, you'd speak true.
But say I've not spoke truth, and you're a fool.

Achilles Returns Hector's Body

No matter how many times I dragged him
around the walls of Troy, he looked alive,
not the maimed mess that would stop my grieving.
I even took a sword to Hector's face,
to no avail; not even the camp butcher's
cleavers and saws, or the boulders I smashed
Hector's head with stopped his sweet, mocking smile.

When his father drove up on a donkey cart,
I snarled, "Return to Troy." He merely stared.
"Speak, old man!" I shouted, the Ancient mute
with grief, tears coursing down his gullied face.
I couldn't bring myself to smash the old fool,
could only recall my Patroclus once
was alive and more beloved than a woman.

And here was this old man, grieving for his son,
and how many bereft fathers cursed me
with the might of a storm tossing a raft?

"Take him," I muttered, but Priam just stared,
tears like stones hurled from a citadel's walls.
"Take him," I shouted, "or you'll join your son!"
Tears hot as a fire's embers etched my face,
and for an instant, I hugged the old man,
as if father and son yoked in mourning.

I escaped into my tent, heard him sigh
and load the corpse onto his cart, the reins
snapping like sails full-bellied in a gale.

From His Tent, Odysseus Watches Priam Take His Son's Body Back to Troy

Too excited for sleep, now that this war
might, at last, end, I watched the cart creak up
to Achilles' tent, Priam soul-weary,
on his knees, begging for his son's body.
I saw the battle within the warrior:
to mock or pity Priam. Kindness won.

But strange, both Priam and Achilles swore
the body wasn't harmed by being dragged,
though I examined the corpse too: mangled flesh,
as if fish had nibbled at it for weeks.
And yet both claimed the face was beautiful,
for which the old man was grateful to Zeus,
and what may have nudged Achilles to kindness:
thinking some god was protecting the man.

Or as likely, Achilles' guilt: for letting
Patroclus wear his armor and get killed;
guilt, too, for savaging Hector in death.
Alive, we feared Hector, especially
after Achilles withdrew in a rage
at Agamemnon—our swaggering king—
demanding Briseis from Achilles,
his own concubine returned to her father.

But now, dead and safe, I admire the man:
defending his country, even if Paris
provoked us by stealing divine Helen;
but just the excuse Agamemnon needed
to launch a war to locust Troy's treasury.

Briseis to Neoptolemus, Son of Achilles:
As Priam Leaves with Hector's Body

There, disappearing into the dawn fog,
the old man and his old maid of a herald:
Kill them both and earn your father's respect.
He lied about returning the body.

Why do you wait? Achilles wants the deed,
but not the pollution of guest killing,
so he's sent the dried-up ass on his way
with what he thinks of as his dearest prize.
But the body will only slow him down.

If you do this one trifling thing for me,
and for your father—whose praise you crave more
than a starving peasant a simple meal—
I'll show you Aphrodite's secret tricks.
And more, you'll finally become the son
your father craves, and thus his rightful heir.

And most important: you, and you alone
will have ended this war successfully,
for how can the Trojans keep on fighting
without Hector, their strongest arm and heart;
and even more, without Priam, their head?

Stop laughing at me, you second-rater.
Don't dare call me Achilles' slattern,
or accuse I enjoyed Priam's cactus.

Honor for a guest? What of the honor
due a woman wronged again and again?
Yes, I'm a witch, so do as I command,
or be careful, my lord, of what you eat.

Melandros, Menelaus' Charioteer, As Priam Leaves with Hector's Body

There goes mighty Hector, who died for Troy,
his beloved home. The fool: home nothing but
a labyrinth of pain to escape from.
I know: my father's sword-flat drunken palms
found my face regular as a lodestone;
Mother's tears endless as Apollo's springs;
and then a wife, and brats screaming, lusty
as nestling griffons for red meat.

Let this war never end, so I'll never
have to return to that cauldron of squalls,
and when my time comes, let me meet it calm
as the swans that still drift in Sparta's harbor:
watching them the only peaceful moments
I could steal from the earthquakes of children
with their greasy, outstretched, tantrumy hands;
my wife, a river of screamed accusations
that I was coupling with Divine Helen.

I laugh: Helen always hissed to My Lord.

I spat on her lineage and beauty;
she ordered Menelaus to beat me,
"And teach the barbarian brute manners."

"No one can drive like Melandros," he countered,
but shot me an arrow-sharp glance of warning.

When she ran away with Paris, I thought,
"Good riddance to tawdry trash," though I knew
Menelaus, the dupe, would never rest
till he'd reclaimed her, exacted tribute
beyond what she was possibly worth.

The one good thing about Hector? He must
have loathed Helen even more than I do.

Menelaus Confronts Achilles After the Latter Returns Hector's Body to Priam

Yes, you slew the man, but as most aggrieved
among the Greeks, I deserve the booty
that scrawny crow, Priam, laid, trembling
at your feet, then escaped into that fog.
Were it me he had dealt with, I'd have taken
the old skeleton hostage, told his slave
to send Helen and Paris with more gold,
and when they arrived, I'd have seized them.

I'd have my fill of Helen, then unleash
my foot soldiers on her: dogs and jackals
snarling over the bones of a lion's feast.
As for Paris, I'd tie him to a burning
wheel, and laugh as flames licked his little man.

When he'd beg for the mercy of swift death,
I'd pour hot vinegar down his gullet,
and keep him alive for days, have slave girls
attend his burns, let him rest, then begin
the tortures again, till that pretty boy was
nothing but a charred slab for circling crows.

Yes, sweet to see him begging, retching, sobbing
at what's to befall him. Maybe I'll force
Helen to deliver the killing knife stroke,
then perhaps I'll take her back, caress her
with all civility: her forever
expecting the blade or my throttling fingers:
she who thought herself above Menelaus,
Lord of Sparta, wealthiest Achaean!

So give me my ransom, great Achilles:
between my brother and me, we're your match.

Agamemnon Joins His Brother Menelaus in Arguing with Achilles

You fool, here's our best chance to end the war.
You men, cut off that wagon; bring it back,
and I'll show you, Achilles, how to bargain.

What, you madman, you're letting it return?
With that corpse and Priam as hostages,
we control the fate of Troy; we set terms
for the city's unquestioned surrender.

Bad enough I was forced to return that bitch
Briseis to you; don't balk me in this.
We can end this war, except for your swearing
that quaint oath and making a bad bargain
with Priam, the old fox, who'd not think twice
about twisting his blade between your ribs.

To make peace with Priam's like appeasing
a pack of wolves, or begging the North Wind
Boreas not to blow our dragon ships
off-course when we finally leave this plain
of death, and return to our homes and wives.

So stand aside now, and let me order
my men—and yours—to pursue that death cart
before it's too late to find it in the fog
that descends like the curtains of green flames
that flicker in the skies above Ultima Thule.

Achilles Confronts Agamemnon and Menelaus

An oath is an oath, and none may break theirs.
I gave Priam my word he could have Hector's
body back, and no matter how you two
thunder, you'll fight me if you wish his corpse.

You, Agamemnon, demanding each Greek
follow your brother in this mad attempt
at Troy, as hard to smash down its stone walls
as the realm of the dead is to escape from.

As for you, Menelaus, always whining
your slut Helen was kidnapped by Paris,
when all the world smirks she gladly ran off
because you paid less attention to her
than to your prize mares, hounds, and all the gems
you fingered, rather than her gorgeous breasts.

I'll carve you both like the sucklings you stuff
into your mouths: greasy as Smyrna figs.
Your golden Helen left you for a younger,
better looking man, who entertained her
with jokes, tales, caresses, not indifference.

Come, both of you, raise your swords like true men.
What, suddenly less enthusiastic
in the grim action than the threatening?
You always were all squawk, strut, and finch-flight.

Diomedes Watches Achilles, Agamemnon, and Menelaus Argue

I never thought Achilles should've denied
the burial. What if his corpse were mangled
by a rage-crazed slayer, one who blamed him
for each wrong done to him and all his kin?

But look at those two fools—Agamemnon
and Menelaus—making to draw swords
against Achilles for returning Hector.
They'll need at least twenty more warriors
to stand a chance; far more sensible, lads,
to put up your swords as fog closes down
and that ox-cart vanishes from your greed.

Still, it's a temptation to see their bellies
pumping crimson: they summoned us to Troy,
then grabbed the biggest share—as our leaders—
of any weapons we stripped from dead foes.
One fight, I used a pair of reins to squeeze
the life from a Trojan who got tangled
in his team's traces: his horses had panicked.

Those Sophists took the chariot and team,
left me his smashed breastplate and shattered spear.
My rage erupted on the unknown corpse,
to my shame: the man suffering enough.

I'd smile to see the Atreides' surprise
they could die so easily, but we need
every fighter to win this mad war: two
matched camps of mindlessly murderous ants.

Nestor Watches Priam Drive Off
with the Body of Hector

I'd have liked to converse with the old man,
cares searing their venom into our faces.
How he got past our sentries, I don't know:
they should've heard him, even in this fog.

I did hear his pleading with Achilles
to free his son's corpse, wisely playing on
both their losses, their lives running away
fast as Mount Ida's spring-melting rivers.

I'd take my blade-flat to Agamemnon
and Menelaus, both of them whining
and threatening when Achilles gave back
Hector's body to the old, mournful king.

They wanted to use the corpse to extract
gems from Priam, as bowmen dip poison
to coat their arrows: doubly treacherous.
I was about to scold the Atreides,
when Achilles drew his perfect bronze sword;
they backed away, as if from Charybdis.
I had to twist my nose to keep from laughing
at their cowering, so blusterful before,
bluffing for the mountain share of booty.

Had Paris not have been blind with Helen,
we'd not have wasted these ten war-hard years.
But how can you tell a father his son
has stirred a cauldron of misery?
Just as well I didn't speak to Priam:
his good son paying for the other's folly.

Thersites, an Achaean Foot Soldier, Watches Priam Leave with Hector's Body

When he finally worked up the lumber
in his gut to face Achilles, he ran
like a hare dodging a wildcat in vain.
From a hill overlooking the plain, we watched,
hoping for a better show from Hector,
ever-noble Hector, hearth-loving Hector:
all the virtues heaped on him, now he's dead.

We Danaans haven't seen our hearths, our wives,
our children in ten years of war, huddling
through winter nights in freezing tents, sweltering
under breastplates and visors in summer
while Trojans feasted, fucked the finest women:
foot soldiers like me denied even hags.

Some swore Hector's defeat was foreordained:
Achilles cheating, near-omnipotent.
But Hector put up almost no struggle,
when what we wanted was the clang of swords,
to see them circle each other, searching
for an opening, a weak spot; wanted
to see Hector's blood, but Achilles' too.

We wanted to see limbs lopped off, a sword's
piercing thud to an enemy's stomach,
his guts spilling out like sausage casings;
a grim head sent flying, stump blood gushing.
We wanted to cheer a skillful kill, not
the humiliation we felt, to watch
a man—considered one of the greatest
warriors—run for his shit-fearful life.

Mouse Hector, masquerading as a hero.

Part II—The Lonely Road Back to Troy

Priam, on His Way Back to Troy with Hector's Body, Thinks of Achilles

I'd slipped a dagger beneath my tunic,
though before we drove away, my wife warned,

"Husband, do nothing to enflame the Greek.
I've lost a son, I'll go mad to lose you.
Dreadful to speak, but I wish Paris was slain;
we could return Helen, and end this war.
To ensure Troy's safety, I'd kill Paris
a thousand times, though you hold the wastrel
closer to your heart than all our better sons.
I was never duped by his beauty, loving
his bright image in any glass or stream.
I wish he'd fallen in, like Narcissus,
trying to kiss his beloved reflection."

"Woman, enough!" I shouted. "I will do
what I must," and slapped the donkey's rump
with the reins, just enough to get it going,
not so sharply that the beast brayed and warned
the Danaan sentinels of my approach.

I was prepared for Achilles' rage,
would use it to slide into dagger range.
I wasn't ready for his grief rivers,
nor for the beauty of my own dead son,
whom I feared would be so mutilated
not even his mother or I would know him.

I stood before the lord of war and wept,
and somehow his stone heart melted as well,
and, through his tears, told me to take my son,
and thus, at least for a while, saved us all.

Verax, a Mule Cart Driver, Upon the Return of Priam with Hector's Body

I'd have gladly driven him, for the love
I bore his son Hector, a man like us,
not like the other royals, eating rich,
while we marched to the fight or sent our sons.

Hector always asked after my brave boys.
After Lendros was killed, Hector himself
bore him to me, kneaded my quaking shoulders
as if he could take all of my anguish.
"Keep your second son safe," he advised me.

I thanked him more than if he'd laid a sack
of gold in my palm, but Kaldros refused.
At each battle, my stomach's in a knot—
like mules gripped by colic—till he returns:
blood drenched, but always some poor Greek bastard's.

So when word spattered—like an evil wind—
Hector had been cut down by Achilles,
I wanted to bring My Lord home to Troy.
But Priam had his herald drive: so scared
he could barely grip the reins. I watched them
creak to the murderous Myrmidon's tent.

After a Hades of waiting, they drove
back through the lower city; we workmen
stood, heads bowed out of respect.
No one breathed or slurped our shared wine,
night dank as swamp bones.

"Should've been that shit Paris," Tul muttered;
we all nodded, and dreamed Hector alive.

Tul the Butcher, as Priam Returns
with Hector's Body

We workmen stood in the thinning dawn mist
as the donkey cart creaked past, all of us
silent and straight as sentries with respect
for Hector, who'd given Troy everything
for ten bloody years, and was now at rest.

I was used to the sight of carcasses,
and I'd wept over my own son's smashed corpse;
but nothing prepared me for poor Hector:
his once noble face now sausage stuffing,
the rest of him mounds of maggoty flesh;
bones cracked apart as if by a lion.
I turned away, but heard Priam remark,

"Thank the gods my dear, dear boy looks himself,
not some festering mass of wounds and gore,"
to slap my head at what I was hearing.

Perhaps in their kindness for Priam's grief,
the gods let him see what he wished to see
and not what was there for all to witness,
sucking in our shocked breaths at the horror
that was passing before us, our caps in hands
out of respect, our eyes cast down, to allow
the grieving king a little privacy.

Threnia, a Prostitute, As Hector's Body
Is Brought Back to Troy

Some gasp his corpse looks fresh as an infant,
some that it's so hacked apart not even
his mother could proclaim, "This was Hector!"
He's dead; who cares if he's whole or in pieces?
All I know, he and his palace kin never
dropped any coins into my hand or bed.

Did I say bed? Nothing so grand as what
he slept on night after cool, perfumed night,
while I cajole brutes to get them to pay
before I go to work on them, their pride
as immense as their pickles are tiny.

You'll ask what did great Hector do to me
that I spit now as his death-cart creaks past?
He did nothing, didn't know I was alive
and frightened, and wished only
to live in peace, and not sell my body
over and over, to every drooler
who squeezes my breasts as if ripe melons,
then shoves his finger into my cavern
to feel how wet and welcoming it'll be.

Hector would proclaim that his palace pals
were fighting for all of great Troy's safety,
so we were bled like pigs for the war's taxes,
when if they'd given that spoiled whore Helen
back to her lawful husband, I'd not have
had to hold Mother when that sergeant croaked
like a raven that Father had fallen,
and none had dragged his body back to us.

The next day Mother rubbed slick crimson paint
into my nipples, showed me how to wear
my robe so men would follow me like hounds,
and whispered what I must do to please them.
When I returned with coins, she lay stiff, cold,
a look on her face begging forgiveness.

Andromache Silently Addresses Hecuba

To hear you, each time Hector drove to war,
I'd hunt up apes who'd escaped the fighting:
a lubricious gibbon, my flaming rump
an inducement to any and all males.

Even if I harbored that vile fondness,
where was I to find a man of such skill
and endowments among the very old,
very young, or very ill and injured
still limping about Troy, trying to find
a rag of sunshine for their exhausted bones,
every healthy man pressed into the fight?

I swear by the virtuous and true gods,
your accusations—wilder than those wretches
possessed by frothing madness—will drive me
to stab you, or myself, in a frenzy.
You hound me about the palace, hoping
to catch me with a courier reporting
to King Priam and his Privy Council,
or with your son Paris; the sight of him
fills me with so many tooth-gnashing sparks
I'm a loom clattering to break apart.

Another man? A regiment of men
that I devour and spit out like grape pips?
I'd laugh if I didn't find it loathsome:
Hector the one man I could let touch me.

My hand reaches to touch him one last time,
even as you, Hecuba, glare and snarl
as if I've stolen a priceless necklace.
Smolder all you want, you evil hag,
I will caress and kiss my darling man,
and if you try to stop me, my dagger
will pierce your wattled throat again and again.

Galatea, a Prostitute, Watches the Body
of Hector Taken to Its Pyre

If I were a liar as well as a whore—
though lies are the core of my profession:
coaxing grunting men into believing
they're the amorous gods' priestly adepts—
I'd sneer that Hector, the great and noble,
was one of my most ardent worshippers,
though his love for Andromache is famous
as the tale of Baucus and Philomen:
who, in death, begged to be metamorphosed
into a holy twining oak and linden.

I only saw him leading men to battle;
and each wretched night fewer chariots
returned, fewer foot soldiers: most bloodied,
bandaged, limping, and some borne on their shields.
You'd think them too spent to toil in my bed,
but the constant threat of death gave them strength.

Then there's Paris, who bids me to grind him.
I could slip a blade between his ribs, display
his head atop Troy's walls, and end this war,
to the cheers of terrified slaves forced to fight.
But by now the Achaeans demand us all dead,
so I suffer his bragging, his tossed coins.

From Hector, I'd not have taken even
a short-weighted drachma: my great honor
to bestow my cunt's temporary joy.
Burn well, My Lord, may your essence flutter
over dread Styx and reside forever
in the meadows of sweet oblivion.

Timal, a Woodcutter, Before the Funeral Rites
for Hector Begin

They say the King beggared the treasury
to get Achilles to give back Hector's body.
Plenty of us that's living what need food:
coins scarce as winter flocks of hummingbirds.
And now, I'm ordered to hew the best logs
for the pyre: my mules weary from dropping off
one load and sent back out for another
by a fat sergeant—you know the siege ain't
making him cut back on meat—his voice a whip.

And when I demand payment, he tells me
it's my civic duty. Duty don't pay
for my wife's, son's, and my mouse-tiny meals.

She doesn't suspect I know why she agreed
to marry me: her palace lover-man
gone like a seagull roving on the wind.
Even if Tamar didn't spring from my seed,
I love him, and my wife, who's not afraid
of hard work, despite her head-spinning beauty,
though it saddens me that each day more wrinkles
weave like spider webs in Luxilla's face.

Still, she'll be prey for every Greek fighter
once Troy's walls are breached, with Lord Hector dead.
If I'm still alive, I'll stand between her
and any that try to violate her,
but they'll have swords; and me, one man with an axe.

As for our son, I just pray he's enslaved,
not have his head bashed in by some raider
what thinks it the greatest joke ever played
to splatter his brains against cobblestones.
By then, I'll be dead, or wishing I was,
even if there's nothing for us poor folk
afterwards but the dark that lasts forever.

Part III—At the Funeral Rites

Jezrius, Court Astrologer and High Priest, Begins the Funeral Rites for Hector

I've examined the entrails of every
imaginable outwardly pure beast,
studied the flights of birds, calculated
the planets' paths—all state one fact: Troy's doomed.

Flames, rape, and murder will spread through our streets
like pools of spilled oil, and Troy will exist
only in stories of our groaning ships;
our bards and artisans the world's envy;
our warriors great as the Immortals:
all, all brought down by Paris, stupid
and stubborn with desire for a slut.

Were there no suitable women in Troy?
My own daughter, her eyes perfect as amber.
In the end, I'm glad his lust led elsewhere:
he'd have had his fill of my Selene,
then tossed her away like a chicken bone.

Now, my one thought's to get my pure daughter
to a port where Troy still has influence.
And when the walls come down—
whether from fires or the dream I forget
upon being thrust from sleep as if shoved
under horses' hooves—I'll slaughter Paris:
easy as slicing the bellies of beasts
to be sacrificed, their innards examined.

Now, my duty's to chant the holy prayers
and set the torch to the logs, to consume
the earthly husk of Hector and waft him
to the Fields of the Blessed, where it's my hope
we shall all meet someday, though I doubt it,
if my examinations are correct:
none alive to place the coins in our hands:

why I must get Selene safe from Troy
as soon as the mourning period's done.

Selene, Daughter of the Court Astrologer

Father wants me safely away from Troy,
but I'll never leave, no matter that he points
to his charts and heavenly measurements,
and swears escape's for my own good.
Good? What do I care for good, when Paris
swears I'm the one woman he's ever loved.

And now that I hide a second secret—
that my belly swells with Paris' love—
he assures me he hopes for nothing more
than to view Helen's corpse, freed from her spells,
her half-enticing, half-sneering, "You're wise
to keep well out of the fighting you started,"
forgetting she was delighted to run
from Sparta with him, rid of her oaf-lord.

"Show me, husband," she taunts, "how brave you are;
prove how much my cunt and Troy mean to you."

But when he storms to strap on his breastplate,
she reveals her glory, and he's her slave,
for which I forgive him, even I tempted
by the goddess-opulence of her beauty:
her titters mocking, "My courageous lord."

I beg him not to listen: he's worth more
alive, and will one day rule over Troy,
with myself as his councillor and wife
once we've disposed of that adder Helen,
nothing more than Menelaus' spy.

Let Father set the torch to Hector's pyre,
let him chant the proper words of farewell,
place the Ferryman's coin in Hector's fist.
But let him stop this talk of my exile:
a blasting curse to me and my great love.

Matax the Pickpocket

Such a caterwauling over one corpse,
when we're all going to be corpses soon.
Time to escape through the secret passage
and ply my trade someplace less dangerous.
But to where? East: barbarian dung heaps.
North: weeks to get anywhere worthy of
my nimble fingers. West? I'd have to steal
a boat and somehow sail to the mainland.
Only South are there cities: my one chance,
if I don't want to end up like Hector.

I'd not have been him for all the lovelies
in Priam's treasury, though his widow
is a looker; not quite Helen, but who'd
choose her and be scorched by her cold, blank gaze?
I've always had to pay for my pleasure:
just as well, no woman to tie me down
with her nagging, and no tantrumy brats.
If I were caught, they'd starve: my hands cut off.

I'll say one thing for Hector's funeral:
the streets are bloated with fat, sobbing marks,
to show Priam and his court their loyalty.
They won't even notice their slit purse-strings.

No, this war won't last long, and when it ends
so will Troy, and anyone caught here: rats
after a harvest, vicious boys unleashed
to have their fun with the killing contests.

It's time to take my chances to the South.
I can pass myself off as a trader
once my own purse is full as the udders
of an un-milked goat. Ah, here's my first mark,
smug to be alive through the tears he sheds
for Hector, and silently curses Paris:
that shiftless hoity-toity believing
every beauty in the world belongs to him.

Cassandra, at Her Brother Hector's Funeral Rites

Father and Astrologer Jezrius
light the logs, and while flames lick Hector's corpse
I see the flames that will eat all of Troy,
but by now, so does anyone with eyes.

I should wait until the palace sleeps, sneak
out in the night fog and run from this war,
from Paris and Helen's tittering self-love;
from Mother, who has less affection for me
than for slipshod kitchen girls more interested
in offering themselves to our heroes
than they are in performing their duties.

I'd leave even Father, who looks at me
with pity for his poor raving daughter.

But there's no escape; I'll sit weeping amid
Troy's smoking ruins, with other women,
Agamemnon smirking for me to follow,
though I'd clawed my face to look like Medusa.

Mother always sneered I'd been given none
of her refined looks or taste, and would scold
no man would desire me. Alas, Mother,
I see a dreadful end, though a spiteful
part of me rejoices that you'll be dragged
down from your throne, debased like all of us.

Drabo, a Trojan Tax Collector

Hector-butchering Achilles? That shit-
pile of greed, Agamemnon? Crow-clever
Odysseus? Cuckoo-horned Menelaus?
Slut-selfish Helen or glass-loving Paris?
No, it's me the populace most desires
to stab some dark night while I make my way
from an inn: drinking so as to forget
not a door will open to me in friendship,
three attempts on my life just this past month.

Why I'm always accompanied by armed men:
Priam demanding more funds for his war
that will live longer than the newborn babe
I beheld suckling at its mother's breast,
blue-veined as a seam of turquoise: her man
a baker, offering her instead of taxes;
I had my guards rough him up a little,
to help him recall where he hid his coins,
while his wife screamed; but oh, the sight of her!

My wife complains she can't venture out
to gossip with other women or visit
the markets and barter for my dinner
because of sword-thrust-glares; she sends her maid,
who always dallies with a palace guard.

While the slut's out, I'm sure my wife's avenging
herself on me with a phalanx of men.
She's refused me all week, so that I'm tempted
to accept that baker's bribe of his darling:
the lovely jade staring as if to say,

"My husband is always smutted with flour.
I long for a clean man, such as yourself."

Trebia, the Mother of a Slain Foot Soldier

Him up there—big man Hector—gets a pyre
and a place of honor in the Blessed Halls,
while my son was ground into bloody dust:
no marker, no monthly wages for me.

Even worse, not knowing if my poor boy
will ever cross the River of Forgetting.
Worse yet: who will put the coin in my hand
when the Gray Sisters cut the cloth of my life?

It's the nobles that always get to sit
in the Halls of Pleasure: here and after;
like him up here, purified by the fire:
a decent sort, or so all the songs tell.
But nothing bad will ever befall him,
nor his brother, bastard Paris, the cause
of this war he can't be bothered to fight.

To him and to his slut Helen, who's more
beautiful without trying than all the whores
that ply their honest trade along Troy's rat-
choked alleys, let the gods grab their coiled tresses
and fling them down to Hades' torments
till they give me back my sweet, loving son!

Zythum, a Crippled War Veteran, Begging at the Funeral Rites

Losing a leg to Achilles' charging
chariot kept me from this eternal war.
Me mates dropped me, screaming, at a saw bones
too drunk to be kin to Asclepius,
but he got the shrieking-grisly job done.

Too bad I didn't marry a pretty whore
to keep me in coins and wine, but women
tire of a man missing a part or two
even if it's not that necessary one.
Still, I earn a day's wage, between leaning
on me crutch, and telling good citizens
all about the fighting, embellishing
a bit, but that's what the punters pay for:
safely behind Troy's wall, too thick to be breached
by even Achilles, thank the gods.

Fat merchants especially generous:
dodging the call-ups, so the clinking coins,
their way of supporting the war effort,
though they moan like wind through Aeolian
harps about being taxed white as lepers.
Whores free with their coins, too, knowing up close
what I went through; after we've done the deed,
I'll sometimes fall asleep, dreams charging me
like Achilles' team: one whore tells me
that's what I scream, when she lets me stay till dawn.

Still, it's not a bad life, better than his
on the pyre, even if he's being rowed
to the Isles of the Blessed, if it exists,
which I doubt; no one ever coming back
to sing its praises, and none in a hurry
to bask in its wine, ambrosia, and maids
more expert at the arts of pleasing men
than the tongue-cunningest daughters of joy
on this side of Lethe's forgetful shore.

Blena, a War Widow

Good riddance to the filthy bastard; not
him burning on the pyre, but my husband,
forever beating me, bringing home whores
to our thatched hut he was too drunk to fix.
At least when he got called up, coins came in,
though he managed—longer than most—to hide
from the battles raging like hurricanes.

Then came the battle he couldn't skulk from,
and afterward, a knock on my rotting
wood door: a sergeant—all muscle—saying
in a voice soft as a fawn, "Your man's gone,
buried on the plain, with the Ferryman's
coin, so you needn't worry he'll wander
the River of Forgetting's barren shore."

He was prepared to catch me if I swooned:
a grieving widow, like so many others.
But I wanted to know about a pension,
and if he had a woman, but was afraid
he'd think me more heartless than Medea.

Instead, it was the Fields of Bliss: gentle
and fierce at once. He came back the next night,
and the next, sighing that time, big and sad
as what him up there, Hector, must've sighed
to have to face that slasher, Achilles:
that at dawn there was another battle,
and he might not make it home from this one,
and left a bag filled with gold, telling me
there was no need to know where it came from.

Fuck the gods for stealing my happiness,
all of it gone with him, though he left me
something else, inside my belly, something
to remember him by the rest of my days.

Hippomanes, Hector's Horse Breaker

What was My Lord thinking of, to take on
invincible Achilles? Worse, Hector
shamed the whole city by running: a mouse
shitting itself to elude a cat's claws.
I'd warned him that to fight the Myrmidon
was futile: the man all but unkillable.

Hector merely strapped on his breastplate, hefted
his spears, tested his sword, and bid me harness
his stallions: unmatched except by the Greek's
immortal mares, more savage in the dust
and blood of battle than wolves that descend
from the blizzard-hills of wintry Thrace.

After I straightened the traces, I looked
into his eyes and saw him searching, praying
for an excuse not to meet Achilles,
but he found only what he deemed his honor.
I never understood this misty honor.

Can one feel its weight like precious gemstones,
caress it like the breasts of one's beloved,
or gaze into it like the proud brown eyes
of the champion stallion one has trained
with a gentle, patient hand and soft words?

No, honor's nothing in this our one life.

Laocoon, Chief of Security, at the Funeral Rites

Our best man dead, still our Scaean Gates tower
like the ice cliffs that guard Ultima Thule.

"Let no one enter," I order the sentries.
"They may look harmless but they hide weapons,
and will murder the whole sleeping city.

I've ferreted every gap in the walls,
every secret passageway, and plugged them
with rocks and mortar; set mastiffs—more fierce
than Cerberus of Hades—to stand guard;
and placed couriers to report any digging.
And still I fear I may have missed traitors
guiding Danaans through forgotten tunnels.

Rumors hissed that one among the helots
was smuggling goods into Troy, after grumblings
the nobles were hoarding all provisions.
I nosed out the traitor, had him gang-pressed
and sent to the front ranks without a fuss.
Since then, I've discovered the gap he used,
have caulked it like the timbers of a ship.
But how many more hidden doors are there?

As chief of security, I should be
inspecting the city, not indulging
my grief at these rites; Great Hector is gone,
but he would warn us—me especially—
to be wary, so I take my leave now,
King Priam staring as if I'm heartless
as a winter storm, when I inform him
I must check our perimeters again.

He's all ceremony; I, all action.
Let history and the bards decide who's
the wiser, more prudent, servant of Troy.

During Hector's Funeral Service, Massopius Tries To Escape from Troy

I searched every inch of Troy's six-foot-thick walls
and finally found the one cranny left.
I'll squeeze through—and escape before the Greeks
scratch their way in like devouring ants—
and vanish into the steppes, leave this war
futile as spiders struggling to climb out
the slick sides of a lantern filled with oil.

I'd risked my one life in twelve battles, knew
the thirteenth would be as ill-fated, for me,
as the wedding of Peleas and Thetis
that set these dread events into motion,
so my searches became more desperate
until I chanced on one unplugged passage,
and widened it bit by bit, so quietly
you'd think I was sculpting a cloud statue.

Now's the perfect time, while all of Troy watches
in hushed sorrow as Hector burns to embers.
I'd nothing against him: a great hero,
loyal to the city; its strong right arm
until the Myrmidon monster slew him.
But we poor foot soldiers were pressed to serve
and die whether we wanted to or not,
and for what? Less likely than my turning
into Theseus that we'd get lucky
with divine Helen, or even be graced
by her smiles, icy as Thracian blizzards.

Better to find a jumble of rough huts
that never heard of Troy and its grand war
that will be sung of forever, because
men will be flung into it, forever.

But now, bastard Laocoon tracks me,
his voice booming for me to surrender,
his great love to keep us all prisoners.
Once I'm through the wall, fuck-all he can do.

Gigantes, a Guard at One of the Secret Passageways in Troy's Wall

Even with my back fully healed, I limp,
and whimper that almost any weapon
is too heavy for me to wield in battle,
so I sit and guard this crack in Troy's Wall,
in case some poor punter tries to escape
under Laocoon's gaze, as jealous
as an old man who suspects his young wife
of giving herself to armies of blades.

He's never caught on that for a small fee
I let masters and slaves pass through, the crack
hidden with easily-shifted shrubbery.

Still, it's getting risky, Laocoon
starting to sniff out there's a leak somewhere.
Why, you might ask, don't I escape as well?
I will, when I've amassed enough drachmas
to live like a king elsewhere, but for now
it's a game of tossed dice: of balancing
having enough, against reckoning when
the Greeks will swarm through in killing numbers.

And what of the women desperate to leave?
Them, I trade with: the juicier ones pay
higher and sometimes with a second fee
before I let them pass, though I don't want
to squeeze then too hard, lest they squawk and fume,
Laocoon's sword ending my pretty business.

So with the whole city mourning Hector,
coins fly into my fist like spawning trout.

Cryptoros, a Greek Spy, at the Funeral Rites

Simple as easing off a maid's drawstring—
to reveal her panting olive-pit nipples—
to sneak in, Troy so proud of its great Wall,
but so many gaps despite the frantic
vigilance of Laocoon: when he plugs
one breach, some enterprising deserter
scratches out another, and not enough
guards to stand sentinel at every gap.

The rest, complacent as grass-cropping sheep;
I can bribe a guard to let our fighters
in one night—silent, deadly as leopards—
the man thinking he'll be able to slip out
once he's performed his treachery. Rule one,
never trust a traitor, slit his throat quicker
than you'd peel an apple, if only I could
remember the tart tang of that crispness
that makes me so pine for home's small pleasures.

Watching them mourn their Hector, I feel pity;
they'll die like lapdogs, shocked at how easy
it was to slip inside and slit their throats,
their women used so hard they'll beg for death.

Trojans sob, and some seem as sick of war
as I was before Achilles gave us hope.
But I see backbone as well, the stubbornness
to fight to the last man; what do I care
that careless Menelaus lost Helen?
I should sneak out, steal a ship, and sail home.

Pyrates, Master Armorer

When I was an apprentice to Father,
I'd carry kindling for the forge, and watch
as he and his assistants tempered swords,
not missing any nuance of the craft:
to my mind the most exalted on earth,
for without our skill, all the other arts
that make life worth the effort are useless.

I beat out my best sword, spear, and breastplate
for Hector when he battled Achilles;
but how was I to know the god Hephaestus
had forged the Myrmidon monster's weapons,
thus giving him an unfair advantage?

Now, some are grumbling it's my fault Hector
ran, knowing his arms were inferior,
his only hope, to make for Troy's great gates.
But I saw he panicked, let my weapons
fall into the fists of our enemy.

King Priam has forbidden me to fight:
too valuable to be wasted in battle;
but should the Danaans ever breach our walls
I'll take as many as I can with me
to the Shore of Death, where, if the Greeks hold
the coin of passage, I'll slice off their hands,
and mock as the silver or gold fee sinks
to Styx's bottom, even as I'll know
none are left in Troy to pay Charon for me.

Noble Hector himself could do no more.

Ilex, the Royal Chef

Forget he was our greatest warrior;
more important to me: the one royal
who never sent back the dishes I served;
ate what was before him and didn't grumble
it was too spicy, not spicy enough,
the meat underdone, overcooked, the sauce
too hot, too tepid, too little, too much.

What did those spoiled nobles expect in war,
the town under siege for ten famished years?
Still, I knew of a few secret tunnels
Laocoon never could figure out,
though he tucks into my succulent dishes
with the gusto of a wild boar, never
considers where they came from, just assumes
they appeared by magic or an answered prayer.

Hector would smile his thanks for any meal:
he should've been a traveling holy man,
a seer, like that blind Tiresias.
When he visited Troy, Paris thought it
a grand joke if a wood stump—masquerading
as a slab of beef—were set on his plate.
Without touching the fake, the blind man chimed,

"Ah, Master Paris, join me in this feast!"
The whole table—even Priam, who loves
the wastrel more than life—broke into laughter.
All except Paris; Priam felt sorry
for the baby, sent him as an envoy
to Sparta, where he stole that bitch Helen,
those two carping loudest against my food.

For Hector, not important what he ate
if it gave him the strength to keep us safe.

Majestius, Court Magician

If I were more than a mere conjuror,
I'd wave my wand and end this weary war,
send the Greeks to Tartarus, then bring back
our lost men, our women who died of grief,
my son and wife the first I'd save from death.

But I'm a mere prestidigitator
performing for the Court's jaded pleasure,
always having to invent ever more
elaborate illusions: not enough
to snap my fingers for doves to appear,
or a coin to grace Helen's perfect ear.
I must seem to slice my slave girl in half:
so little room for error, or her blood
will summon all the demons of Hades.

Hector, you should've killed Paris the instant
he preened off his ship, parading his slut
as if a prime broodmare, when everyone
knows she's barren as my bright illusions,
even if she's a goddess of beauty.

Beauty's nothing more than yet another
illusion that will fade with the hard glare
of years and worries that not even true
sorcerers can wave away with their wands.

Dinaros, a Second Beggar

I wasn't so foolish as to let myself
be pressed into this war: coming through it
unscathed more hopeless than trying to hide
once your Fate's been stitched, measured, and snipped short.
Instead, I poked out my eyes: robins' eggs
evil lads splat from a high tree-limb nest.

My bitch-hearted wife used that as an excuse
to leave me for that oaf of a butcher,
a brute too dull to see how she plays him
like the strings of a fine-crafted lyre.
She knew I was too clever, even blind,
not to see, or sniff, what she was up to
with others, so she ditched me like a puppy
you'd toss into a stream, and found that dolt.

I've traded the pick-pocket trade for begging,
safer, the punishment, to lose both hands.
I let folks think I lost my eyes in war,
and women coo at my cunning fingers.

And I don't have to hear my wife's nagging—
the caw of a crow that won't stop its taunting—
that if I loved her I'd find fancy digs,
and buy her the most fashionable robes.

That butcher? She'll bleed him like a drained hog.
And I'm still alive, though him, brave Hector,
up there on that pyre, ain't. You want to know
real bravery? Jabbing that blade in one eye—
the pain making me faint—then the other.

Pepella and Her New Husband, a Butcher

When this war began, I still sucked my thumb,
wore child-bright ribbons in my hair, and held
Papa's workman's hand: hard as his heart was soft.
When he'd chat with men in the agora,
he called me the prettiest girl in Troy;
I was, am now, a wonder of beauty:
wasting it on my first husband, a thief
turned self-blinded beggar: desperate with fear
he'd be press-ganged into Hector's army:
loving his wee life more than he loved me.

Papa died of grief—Mama long ago—
when I agreed to marry Dinaros,
attracted by his profession's peril,
and by the way he'd smile, his crooked tooth
gleaming like a wolf's fang, and that small scar
above his left eye, and I'll admit it,
the bulge I could see beneath his short-robe.

They say it's only a matter of time
before the Greeks breach the walls and slaughter
all the battle-age men, make the women
slaves, if we're alive after they've used us.
I'll not wait for the Greeks: tonight, with all
of Troy attending the rites for Hector,
I'll perform such tricks on my swine-husband,
he'll reveal the one secret tunnel left.

The brute's so trusting he'll hand me the blade
I'll slit his throat with, then set out alone
for freedom beyond these walls closing in
on me like a magic crushing chamber
Daedalus might fashion for Crete's beast-king.

Crillus, a Dead Trojan Foot Soldier
and Brother to Baicus the Tavern Owner

Brother, when the press gang shattered our door,
you hid, while I was dragged off like a goat
to be sacrificed to the gods, but slobbered
and belched over by Priam's priests instead.
You were always the practical one: married,
putting in long hours serving barleyed wine
to foot soldiers desperate for refreshment
after the battles; and glad to offer
wenches to help them forget the curses,
blood, screams, shattered bones when chariots
thundered, as if whipped by indifferent gods.

As for me, I was the fun-loving one,
who'd not be tied down by a wife, children,
or your wine and wench-soggy tavern.
And my secret? Your wife and I met once.
Doomed lovers, we moved like a mad typhoon
crashing black waves against a rocky shore.

Both of us sweating, panting like coursing hounds,
we vowed to run off; but next night press gangs
smashed down the door. Did you call them, Brother?
When I was dragged off, I saw you smirking;
a sergeant shoved a sword into my hand,
then a Danaan spear-thrust and I was dead.
But I thank you for finding my body
before the dogs did, for carrying me back
to your tavern, and cleaning me off yourself.
I thank you too, for the coin and the pyre
to burn off impure flesh, for my crossing.

When you join me, will we know each other
or glide past, only wraiths? I'm forgetting
your face, what games we'd play when we were kids
and you had to win or you'd flatten me.
Worse, I'm forgetting Memna, how she'd brush
against my arm with her breasts while whispering,

"Be patient, my love, it won't be long now."

Memna, Wife of the Tavern Owner Baicus

I lied that I wept for fallen Hector.
It was for your war-slain brother I sobbed.
Husband, we've been wed for more than three years
and never have I felt new life's stirring.
Then Crillus, your younger brother, snuck back
from his latest adventure beyond Troy,
his mysteries a love potion: I'd brush
his arm with breasts that ached to burst with milk.

The night you were called away on business,
I invited Crillus to warm our bed.
Oh, such a night I'll never know again:
comets flashed, the lights men who travel north
to Ultima Thule report seeing, swirled
emerald curtains across the sky bowl,
Zeus' lightning bolts sizzled over and over.

All day, we tried to act as if nothing
had burst between us and planned our escape,
but you went out again, and that evening
as we were about to send home the last
drinkers, in burst the press gang, claiming Crillus.
You paid them, didn't you? Promised them girls
for free, and of course, wine, within reason:
always more miserly than a spider.

Now Crillus is dead and I sob, and tell you
it's for great Hector my tears pour like wine
from a knife-slit sack. Tonight, I'll let you
give me succor, though I'd sooner stab you.
I'll make sure you succeed, in case Crillus
has beaten you and planted his own spy—
wilier than Greek Odysseus—in me.

After the Funeral, the Tavern Owner Baicus
Thinks About His Wife and Dead Brother

As we watched and wept at the lapping flames,
it hit me like a leather-covered fist:
it wasn't for noble Hector she sobbed,
but for Crillus. I could throttle Memna.

Am I that unpleasing in appearance?
Am I a brute, a beater of women?
Have I not given her all that she wants?
All I know: this morning I grieved Crillus'
death as if my heart had been ripped apart,
worshipped Memna like Hera, Queen of Heaven.

Now I curse my wife to black Tartarus.
As for my brother, I wish he'd wander
Styx's near bank and grieve his treachery.
I did nothing but love him and boast of
his courage: smuggling supplies into Troy:
a hero to us poor folk, nobles grabbing
most of the meat and produce, tossing us
a few gleaned corn cobs from their granaries.

Now she plucks at my cock like a zither,
proof she carries Crillus' bastard get.
She mocks me, and I, her eternal fool,
arise to her caresses. May brigands
ravage her, may Charon spit in her face
and laugh at her: only, not tonight.

Priam's Prayer: The Last Day of Mourning

My son, forgive me; I never gave you
enough credit: accepted your goodness,
your duty and courage as merely my due.
And worst of all, I loved, love, Paris more.
My son, you're going to the Blessed Fields,
where you'll sit in ease, while bards sing your deeds;
don't, I beg, forget us, as the dead do.

I fear we shall all be joining you soon,
should the Ferryman's coin be given us.
But what if Troy be wiped out, nothing left
but blowing sand and corpses for hungry dogs?
We'll moan forever on Styx's near shore;
if you've the ear of the gods, remind them
of our griefs, our losses, our righteous lives.

If you can't do this for me, then at least
for your mother, wife, son, your brother Paris.
Yes, a wastrel most selfish in his lusts,
but my fault, giving him all he desired.
I ignored his drinking, his gaming, sanctioned
his stealing Helen, and look where that led:
this war that will end with our unmourned slaughter.

Your mother keeps your ashes by her,
whispers to them, strokes the urn, causing me
to fear her mind's scattered with blizzard grief.

If you have any feeling for her, beg
Zeus to let us join you, when it's our time.

Hecuba Answers Priam's Plea
to Their Dead Son Hector

"Husband, far better had you loved Hector—
the more worthy son—than plead with him now.
It's unseemly, craven to beg for safe passage
for all of our remaining family.

"Cease this useless whine: Hector can't hear you,
can't even recall he had a wife, father,
son, self-loving brother and slut sister,
let alone a mother who would've slaughtered
the whole world to keep him safely by me.

"Reclaim the dignity I loved you for:
call up more reserves, shore up our ramparts,
make sure no Greeks—led by traitors—can squirm
through the Walls' secret passages and cracks.
Send out spies and night patrols to harass
their sentries, burn their weapons and grain stores.

"Even without my Hector, the Greeks will never
beat us in battle. What we must guard against
is a scheme that makes us think they've gone home,
when they've merely found the back way to Troy.
That's better, dear husband. It lifts my heart
like a hawk on the good-omen right-side
of the sky to behold you firm again."

By Hera of the stout-souled marriage oath,
what did I ever esteem in that mouse?
Overnight a trembling, dithering ancient
wanting only his bowl of hot porridge
as he sits and shakes by a winter fire.
I should slit his throat, rule in my own name,
and let the gods take pity on Paris
and Helen, for I will most surely not.

Andromache, on the Last Day of Mourning

Until I saw the pyre's flames licking you
like a great, hungry cat, I truly thought
you'd stand up from your blazing, oil-soaked bed
and walk down to me and Astayanax,
that we'd stroll away from Troy's charnel house,
and find some quiet hinterland cottage
to live out our contented days, watching
our son grow to be a peaceful shepherd,
safe from court intrigues and eternal war.

I'd tend our garden, you'd cultivate grapes
and stand sentry over our flocks of sheep.
In Time's kindness we'd be joined by our son's
sweet wife, then grandchildren to whom you'd give
horse-rides on your knees, while they'd shriek delight.
We'd fall asleep after our good day's work:
me with a needle and wool in my hands,
you mending a sandal: "No sense in waste,"
you'd say, not like a royal prince of Troy.

The fancy so fragrant I'd closed my eyes
to see and enjoy its balm more clearly:
beholding our lives, our deaths zephyr-serene,
changed into a pair of immortal doves
or twining trees, together for all time.
I opened my eyes, expecting to see
that placid meadow of our grazing flocks.

But your pyre crackled, tears gouged down my face;
without thinking, I drew my viper blade,
to make the red slash and join you in death.
But that meddler Paris stopped my knife thrust.
I beat his chest with my fists, tried to scratch
his eyes out, but others dragged me away,
when all I wanted was to be with you.

Trema, Servant to Andromache

I shrieked when My Lady slid her bright blade
from its pretty sheath and tried to slash herself.
Luckily My Lord Paris grabbed the knife
while she stormed such curses I never thought
to hear from a princess of the royal blood:
for denying her passage to her husband,
for Paris causing this war. I'd forgive him
for one smile: more handsome than Apollo.

All very well for her to end her woes
with a little dagger-prick, but what of her child,
who dances in his crib when she approaches?
Had she deserted him to me, I'd be under
Queen Hecuba's appraising lizard-eye:
"Madam Sneer and Scowl." For her, nothing's ever
good enough, 'specially not from servants:
when it's us that keep the palace running
smooth as a hollowed gourd of fresh goat's milk.

Us servants never have time to think
about ending it, too busy seeing
to the Quality's whims, though I'll say this:
Andromache's a better mistress than most,
never asks me to do nothing she'd not
do herself, unlike La-Di-Dah Helen,
who lolls in her chambers, traipses along
the ramparts for all to suck in our breaths
at her beauty, snapping her delicate fingers
like she owned the palace and all of us,
and not here on Paris' sufferance.

Us who serve in this life will have to do
the same in the next, so what's the great rush,
if it's going to be, "Do this, fetch that"?
I'll stick it out here, and if Lord Paris
stumbles drunk into my pallet some night,
I'll guide his best part to my nice warm nest.

After Andromache's Outburst,
Cassandra Holds Astayanax

Poor, wee Astayanax, come to my arms.
No one ever listens to what I say,
so I'll not shriek Troy will be breached, your small
body flung against a wall, broken into
a hundred bloody shards, to keep the House
of Priam from ever rising again.

I'll care for you until Mama's herself,
despite Grandmama's sneers: confusing frost
for strength. Just look at Grandpa's cowering:
a miracle he reclaimed Hector's corpse.

"You're a fool," she scalded, "if you believe
you'll return alive, let alone with my son.
Greeks will scythe you like a blade of barley."
When he drove back with Hector's corpse, it was,
"Why didn't you kill Achilles as well?"

You might say this war made her as bitter
as the poisons the centaur Nessus mixed
to avenge himself against Herakles,
but she always possessed that burning tongue.
Woe to us, her children, if we dared speak
while she belittled Papa's competence.

All except Hector, whom I should've hated
for being so loved, but he shielded me
from her rages, though even he didn't believe
the premonitions that wracked me like wind
through withers-high grass on the eastern steppes.

The visions scream again: flames licking Troy,
Danaans bursting in; swords, death everywhere.

Part IV—The War Goes On

After the Funeral Rites,
the Deserter Threnon Faces Execution

The clever ones sneak out during the night
through the Wall's fissures, the city asleep,
but I cast off my shield and tried to dash
from the battle: unable to bear the war
any longer, my palms sweaty to grip
my spear and shield, the thunder of Danaan
chariots making me piss my loincloth.

So I ran, into the arms of a sergeant.
In my terror, I struck and slew the man;
others gave chase and dragged me back to Troy,
tossed me into a cell and forgot me
till Hector did his own running, when all
recalled I'd made a widow and orphans:
me, with no one to shed tears for my death.

It was decreed my execution would not
pollute the sacred rites for holy Hector,
but once the twelve days of mourning were done,
I'd be taken out and finished with a sword:
my blood an offering to appease the gods
and to grant us victory, despite losing
our greatest fighter, our most noble man.

Now, my hands bound like sticks to feed a fire,
I'm forced to kneel, but I'm shaking so hard
the executioner kicks me in the ribs
to still me, and all I can do is pray
to Father Zeus I'll wake from this foul dream,
and find myself walking the road away
from Troy to someplace peaceful; and there meet
a wench, our bed-battles fierce, but harmless.

Bathyros, Hector's Former Squire

I'll kill the man who lies brave Hector ran.
What looked like panicked retreat was really
his trying to wear out Achilles, before
he pivoted like a leopard pursued
by wolves, snapping the spine of the closest,
tearing into the others of that snarling,
craven pack, complacent in their numbers.

That was his plan, only the Greek monster
employed some unscrupulous ruse and cut
down My Lord before he could end the war
with one stroke of his sun-flashing sword.

I loved My Lord Hector for plucking me
from a brought-low family: Father losing
our fortune on gaming, reckless with wine:
after Mother died, Father's heart shattered.

One day, Master Hector sat with Father
and passed him a pouch, then beckoned to me.
To my shame, I cast only a quick glance
at Father, who caressed his cheap wine bowl
like the beehive breast of an eager whore.
My official training began next dawn,
Lord Hector grooming me to replace him
as the champion defender of Troy.

So it's my duty to avenge My Lord;
I might look slight, still a youth, my hair blowing
into my eyes, my forearms not nearly
as rope-thick as my great Lord Hector's were,
but a sinewy power of purpose.

Let Achilles slice me for the vultures,
I'll never, never stop coming at him,
be it on Troy's plain or the mists of Hell.

Kallindros, Hector's Chariot Driver

It shames me to remember that My Lord,
challenged, ran like a child from night demons.
This shame will not leave me, though I take drink
in a tavern; other drinkers taunt me,

"Where's your magnificent Lord Hector now?
What good was all his duty and honor
when he couldn't stand against Achilles?
Any of us could've run from him too,
but we expected better from the best
man we Trojans had to throw at the Greeks."

I stop their sneers for an instant, my dagger
pinching the loudest one's throat, then find silent
respite with a whore who'd not mock My Lord.

I've been reassigned to drive another
spearman, not nearly the fighter My Lord
Hector was, but he has the look of one
who knows how to stay safe; maybe we'll make
it through this war with our breath inside us,

all I hope for now; and the whores I climb
each night, forgetting, if just for a moment,
this war and the way My Lord Hector ran.

Adriana, Helen's Maid

Through the days of mourning for Lord Hector—
our rock, our wall—she was virtue itself:
modest in grief; never the butterfly
she'd been ever since that first time she glanced
into her glass and gasped at her beauty,
as have all men and women ever since.

But now that the war rears up again
like a stallion that will not be broken,
she flaunts herself before Trojans and Greeks.
Paris—chastened as a small boy caught stealing
some treat from a trusted cook and blaming
the poor man—vows to defend the city.

"Excellent," she mocked. "I'll amuse myself
with other, more pleasantly ardent men."
A daemon possesses her, and nothing
I say—while I curl her tresses—can stop
her sneering, high-born courtesan laughter.

"What will become of you," I barely dare
to breathe while she examines my handiwork
in her glass, "should the Danaans breach the wall?
Surely they'll kill you, for running with Paris."

I dare not mention my fear for myself,
for we servants count less than loyal dogs
in the affairs of our lords and ladies;
they expect us to throw ourselves upon
the bronze swords of invaders for their sakes.

"I have but to glance at them, and the oafs
will fall to their knees and beg forgiveness.
Look at me, Adriana. Could anyone
resist me?" My hand reached to stroke her face;
it was stopped only by her witch-tittering.

Limnos, Paris' Servant, After the Days of Mourning

When great Hector's corpse was returned to Troy,
My Lord foreswore carnal games with Helen.
But as he stood, head bowed, I saw him bored,
a sullen brat wishing to be at play.

Some in my place would chafe to be servant
to brave Hector, but I'm out of the fighting,
get to ogle Queen Helen, though as much
chance of my bedding that divine strumpet
as a slug being kissed by Artemis.

Palace staff hiss Helen brought ruin to Troy:
one jade muttered, "I'd toss her off the ramparts."
"But first," a male attendant laughed, "I'd take
my pleasure upon her goddess-body."

Still, I must thank that smirking queen of lust:
her servant and I started with hot glances,
then progressed to brushing innocent hips.
We've found some privacy in the stables,
my dear whispering, "I've learned her love tricks."

If I'd been Hector's man, I'd have trembled
for my future: a sinking pond pebble.
Instead, my duties are as little taxing
as a boy too young to bring in the cows.
I lay out My Lord's robes, and if he rouses
himself to fight, I clasp on his breastplate
and watch him drive out, and pray he returns,
so I won't be reassigned to a more
demanding lord; or, the gods forbid it,
have a rotting shield shoved against my chest,
and commanded to stand in the front ranks.

Epilogue

The Ghost of Hector Bids Farewell

At dawn, the killing will begin again
while I'll drift in wraith-mist past Styx's shore
and forget this world and its joys and pain:
Not Andromache, I pray, just this war.

I fought for love of Troy, our only home,
and kept the Greeks at bay for ten hard years,
while crows and vultures fed, and wild dogs roamed,
and tore at the wounded, eyeless with fear.

The night before I died, I sensed my end,
but a man must face death with cheerful heart;
what warriors learn, or at least pretend:
the code we live by that sets heroes apart.

But if I had it to do once more,
I'd have slain Paris and his fucking whore.

Acknowledgments

The author wishes to thank the editors of the journals listed below, in which the following poems, some in earlier form and some with slightly different titles, first appeared:

Classical Outlook: "Achilles Wakes from a Dream of Patroclus," "Menelaus Confronts Achilles After the Latter Returns Hector's Body to Priam," "Thersites, an Achaean Foot Soldier, Watches Priam Leave with Hector's Body," "Ilex, the Royal Chef," "Matax, the Pickpocket," "Priam's Prayer: the Last Day of Mourning," "Verax, a Mule Driver, Upon the Return of Priam with Hector's Body," "Andromache Silently Addresses Hecuba," "Galatea, a Prostitute, Watches the Body of Hector Taken to Its Pyre," "Selene, Daughter of the Court Astrologer"

Ekphrasis: "Timal, a Woodcutter, as the Funeral Rites for Hector Begin"

Iconoclast: "Diomedes Watches Achilles, Agamemnon, and Menelaus Argue," "Nestor Watches Priam Drive Off with the Body of Hector"

Illuminations: "Tul the Butcher, as Priam and His Herald Idreus Return with the Body of Hector," "Majestius, Court Magician"

NEBO: "Dinaros, a Second Beggar," "Pepella and Her New Husband, a Butcher"

U.S. 1 Worksheets: "Achilles Returns Hector's Body"

About FutureCycle Press

FutureCycle Press is dedicated to publishing lasting English-language poetry in both print-on-demand and Kindle formats. Founded in 2007 by long-time independent editor/publishers and partners Diane Kistner and Robert S. King, the press was incorporated as a nonprofit in 2012. A number of our editors are distinguished poets and writers in their own right, and we have been actively involved in the small press movement going back to the early seventies.

Each year, we award the FutureCycle Poetry Book Prize and honorarium for the best original full-length volume of poetry we published that year. Introduced in 2013, proceeds from our Good Works projects are donated to charity. Our Selected Poems series highlights contemporary poets with a substantial body of work to their credit; with this series we strive to resurrect work that has had limited distribution and is now out of print.

We are dedicated to giving all of the authors we publish the care their work deserves, offering a catalog of the most diverse and distinguished work possible, and paying forward any earnings to fund more great books. All of our books are kept "alive" and available unless and until an author requests a title be taken out of print.

We've learned a few things about independent publishing over the years. We've also evolved a unique and resilient publishing model that allows us to focus mainly on vetting and preserving for posterity poetry collections of exceptional quality without becoming overwhelmed with bookkeeping and mailing, fundraising activities, or taxing editorial and production "bubbles." To find out more about what we are doing, come see us at futurecycle.org.

The FutureCycle Poetry Book Prize

All original, full-length poetry books published by FutureCycle Press in a given calendar year are considered for the annual FutureCycle Poetry Book Prize. This allows us to consider each submission on its own merits, outside of the context of a traditional contest. Too, the judges see the finished book, which will have benefitted from the beautiful book design and strong editorial gloss we are famous for.

The book ranked the best in judging is announced as the prize-winner in January of the subsequent year. There is no fixed monetary award; instead, the winning poet receives an honorarium of 20% of the total net royalties from all poetry books and chapbooks the press sold online in the year the winning book was published. The winner is also accorded the honor of being on the panel of judges for the next year's competition; all judges receive copies of the contending books to keep for their personal library.

www.ingramcontent.com/pod-product-compliance
Lightning Source LLC
Chambersburg PA
CBHW070009100426
42741CB00012B/3174